# Falling in Caves

## Diane Kistner

**FUTURECYCLE PRESS**
*Mineral Bluff, Georgia*

Published by FutureCycle Press
Mineral Bluff, Georgia, USA

ISBN 978-1-938853-37-1

# Contents

The Cave of Dreams...................................................................... 7

Mixing Metaphors...................................................................... 8

Bare Feet: Europe in a Fit of Downs........................................ 10

Karen............................................................................................ 13

On Bus With Bibleman.............................................................. 14

Father and Son............................................................................ 16

Surveillance................................................................................ 19

Eight Sets by the Sea................................................................. 20

The Walls...................................................................................... 22

Fable for Fools............................................................................ 24

Ten Vain Attempts..................................................................... 26

The Mask...................................................................................... 29

Oneself.......................................................................................... 30

One's Gift..................................................................................... 31

Shell.............................................................................................. 32

Childhood's End......................................................................... 35

Falling in Caves.......................................................................... 36

Ghost Town, Mill and White.................................................... 38

Nymph.......................................................................................... 39

The Lamps of Night................................................................... 40

Hide and Seek............................................................................. 42

Acknowledgments...................................................................... 43

*for Robert*

## The Cave of Dreams

Who are you, clothed in sleep's thick wool—
soul or shade or shadow, maven, man—
who grabs me by the hair, hurts me,
drags me through the dirt;
who shows me the magic paintings
on the dark walls of this cave?

# Mixing Metaphors

## I.

It comes again,
this buzz in the head,
this thread I spin out to guide me
through the maze.
I weave in,
converse with the Minotaur,
that memory I have locked away so well.
It is ugly, a family embarrassment.

## II.

A white thread will go through any eye,
eyes of peacocks, cyclones, evil,
eyes of agates, cats,
my own eyes.

## III.

I want to leave all the hems hanging,
the offending threads trailing the floor.
This perpetual pain of proper impressions:
each stitch a thought I've lost,
a diversion, a pricked finger.
The hem of each dress,
the chin of each face
bears a trace of blood.

## IV.

The forest is darkest
when night falls down.
I leave a trail of crumbled bread
to the edge of it.
I cannot return to my father's house.
No more can I feel the comfort
of his arms.
Hungry, full of dread,
I am easy prey.
I stumble,
sightless as the night,
frightened by shadows
of shadows
of my own shadows.

## V.

Tomorrow, if birds
have not eaten all the crumbs,
I hope to thread my way out
of this maze, this forest.

## Bare Feet: Europe in a Fit of Downs

Shoes without feet will not go anywhere,
      will sit in their display cases
    singing songs of no mud.

I often wonder about the empty bottle
      on the nightstand.
Has it become me?
Has it a place to go and feet to walk in?

Oh, the light from a Spanish window,
      the burn of a belly that knows no end
    to its asking!
Looking, I can see the dead dry olives
      spit out on the floor.

We are not going anywhere, my feet and I.
We are not going anywhere.

You, dog on my bed,
      you think you have a right to be here.
Your hairs stick
      to my antelope-suede jacket
    like ticks in your coat
    who really believe they have a right to be here.

And don't they?
Spanish moss hangs from oaks
    in Florida;
    bums sleep on sidewalks
      next to the university;

my fingers rattle the shaky keys
  of someone else's typewriter.

If you fly away far enough,
    if you get in a hole full of papers,
    if you chin up onto the highest roof in your town,
    *something* will see you long enough
      to shoot you down.

You never know who could be admiring you
      from a distance.
  Two blocks down in the pharmacy
  there is a mirror that I will never look into
      as long as I live.

My womb is wandering again.
The dog on my bed is scratching fleas.
My bones could be rattling for all I know;
      I have no more keys,
    and the sticks and rotten oranges outside my window
      have stopped asking the time.
They have their flies when the sun is hot,
    and I have a dog's fleas sucking my spine.

If I turned out the light,
                    no one would be here.
I look at the bottle again,
    wishing its warm tongue into my belly.

My shoes thrown in a corner are black and serious.
Perhaps they will get up
    and walk me to Russia.

Perhaps they will walk me
    into Africa's deep black bowels.

Perhaps they will walk me home.

Shoes without feet will not go anywhere,
    will sit remembering their little glass houses
        empty as the inside of a bottle.

My feet are bare and shivering
        like an old man's head emptied
    and Indian-skinned.

# Karen

There are horses on Karen's walls.
There are dolls in the closet
staring their dreams out like dogs
in the dark of an alley.

Karen's boots stiffen in a corner.
Blue ribbons over the mirror fade.
A desk calendar remembers her birthday
the third year in a row.

If a hand would come down,
would trace the rooms dust edges,
it might find a porcelain rider
on a horse with broken legs.

But no one comes here anymore,
not since they locked the door.
There are horses on Karen's walls,
horses she thought raced on wings.

## On Bus With Bibleman

Last night witches broomed the sky,
       harvest moon sweeping,
   darking the suede-smooth light.
Splashed with that bold Octobering,
     the oaks stood, choked with autumn's paint.

I knew the Bibleman would come.
When maples are colored orange and silver
    and the air smacks
       with all the indifference of squirrels,
    the dogwoods silently stain their leaves
       with blood.

First time he boarded my bus
      it seemed odd that his mouth
   screwed into his face that way,
      odd that his coat smelled of nightwolves.
A symptom of the season, I thought,
    like runny noses and neck scarves.

Autumn swept the bus like disease:
      geese winging in old men's frowns,
   gossips clattering like brown leaves
     blown down a dead-end street.

At the fare box coins clunked
      and there he stood grinning pumpkin-awkward,
   his hair cropped churchyard close,
     and a thin white Bible lodged,
   stark as a tombstone,
      in the muddy green of his coat.

Rumpled-quiet he sat, head lowered, eyes closed.
You could hear the bus breathing.
Then came the muttered, muffled prayers,
        mutterings, head-bobbings,
    warts on his fingers like frogs.
A red ribbon wilted in the New Testament
    like altar flowers on Wednesday.

He must have been thinking of Jesus.

## Father and Son

Theirs were the same blue eyes
      flashing fire from the roots,
   theirs the heavy grinding in the throat.
My son grew tall,
      grew strong as the sun-browned farmhand
   who came to work hay each year,
   and his hair was as gold as the hay
      out by the barn
   with a wild moon on it.

I was a wild, laughing girl,
      fifteen and pretty,
   wife of the man with the big farm
   down by the river.
A dwarf of a man he was,
      a man of God's law,
   a man whose heart couldn't dance
   in the barn at hay-cutting.

*Those gold-fevered nights*
   *when I left his bed to dance!*

There were quiet nights by the fire
      when the hay was all cut.
I would watch them, my son
      and this man of my father's choosing,
   would watch them for years
   while the lie settled my wild heart
      like Georgia river mud.

A dark, quiet bit of a man he was
      beside my son, *my* son
   with the moon's kiss in his eyes.

*Those gold-fevered nights*
   *when I left his bed to dance!*

One day they went into the forest early,
      him swinging the sun-sharp axe.
   "Back after dinner," he said.
   "Enough wood to burn out winter."
I watched them walk away side by side,
      my son in his sixteen years
   and that dark, quiet man
   no taller than a farmhand's shoulders.
Lord, I watched them sink into the forest
      black as the lie.

There beside the roughing Chattahoochee,
      quick, aloof as old Indians,
   the axe fell again and again.
And there he lies, dogwood-mangled,
      hands twisted in ten awful questions,
   the ground stained there, the moon-golden head
   hewn from the oak of my boy.

*He* did no wrong.

A wise Baptist-preaching southern man,
      he saw in my son's proud trunk
   his crookedness mirrored to death,

saw the nights of magic and barn dance
      and all the cheap silver of my betrayal.
Like a god in the anger of his genes,
      he righted all wrongs to him,
    made the lie holy and whole,
    carved my son in his own image.

# Surveillance

You have placed your eyes
in all the trees
to watch me as I walk,
alone
or not alone
through the garden.

Your eyes are so small
they are almost invisible,
but I see them,
hundreds,
watching like tiny insects.

I slip my shoes off
by the pool,
step out of my summer dress.

The water is cool
against the sky's rude blueness.

# Eight Sets by the Sea

**I.**

Sponge-thick foam encircles the island.
Black and orange fishes
    dart among the corals.

**II.**

I watch the sea wash the beach's body.
If I looked long enough,
    I could see the seaweed drown.

**III.**

When the sea rushes back,
    a part of the sound remains
    puddled on the rocks.

**IV.**

In the sun the rocks burn black.
In the sun the rocks glare
    like empty mirrors.

**V.**

Crabs sneak across the face
    of the beach
    like painted fans.

**VI.**

The air leans upon the sand.
My hands scoop up the hours,
    the scattered, speckled shells.

## VII.

From the west, the only wind
    blows from the wings of a seagull.
Crushed in its beak, a spotted snail
    grows larger.

## VIII.

In the scarlet ear of a shell
    I can hear our mother
    speaking to the moon.

# The Walls

*for my mother*

Four years old
with colored crayons,
you have discovered the walls.
Not old enough yet
to know better,
you have covered the white expanse
of your boundaries
with castles
and kings and queens
from your Mother Goose book.
You have walked
in your own enchanted forest.
You have flown bright flags
against a sky of dreams.
You have skipped down
to a sea of fishes,
splashed upon the beach,
built castles of sand
and danced
and laughed
when the waves
washed your castles away.
Crayon in hand
and queen of your land,
you believe
you can always make more.

When I spank you,
you cry and hate me
and stare with those dark
yet not extinguished eyes.
I wash and wash
at your pictures
with soap and rags,
trying to make the walls dull
and white again.
How long will it be
before you stop fighting me,
I who am grown up
and see all colors at once,
undone, whirled
into oneness?
How long will it be
before you accept
the walls?

## Fable for Fools

*for Kay*

I don't want to see you anymore,
you with those eyes,
you with that black hibachi
of burning coals.
We've had our picnic.
We've had our day of crumbs
and ants in the grass.
I sat, as always, glad to be with you.
You told a borrowed story by the lake:
*In winter, the foolish grasshopper,*
*who labors all the summer making song,*
*will starve or freeze to death in the snow.*
The dogwoods were so white then,
the ducks and swans so white,
that nothing could seem cruel
or break the spell.
I sat, arrested by your eyes,
on fire as they always were
with one of your tales;
and your hair, which was black
and arresting too,
flashed and crackled in the sun's white light.

Oh, then the day was warm
and there was food.

Ants were all over us.
*An ant,* you said, *is enduring, strong,*

*can carry ten times its weight*
*on its back at once.*
I had no love for the ants,
nor should I now.
I watched them crawling over the cloth
to plunder our basket of food,
their small black bodies crackling in the sun,
and I listened, not really to you,
for the locusts sang in the trees!
You admired them only as symbols, you said,
symbols for fools:
*Only the hardened ants can survive the winter.*
But the day was so warm
that nothing could seem cruel,
and the locusts sang,
and I was singing,
and swans were crossing the lake,
and light spilled down
like the beard of a sage, in waves
white and concealing.

## Ten Vain Attempts

**I.**

I don't want to leave my apartment
because I know my anger
will want to go out with me.
Afraid of that,
I decide to stay at home.

**II.**

I light candles in every room
and window,
hoping that the light
will deny my anger.

**III.**

I burn a chicken in the oven.
I serve it to myself
with a glass of vinegar
as punishment for my anger.

**IV.**

I stare at my face
in the bathroom mirror,
trying to outstare
the face of my anger.

**V.**

I make a small coffin
out of a cereal box.
I paint the coffin red and black.

I kill a spider and bury it
in the yard,
pretending that the spider
is my anger.

## VI.

I strike a match
and watch it burn
slowly
down to my fingers
I strike a second match
and watch it burn
down to my fingers.
I strike a third,
a fourth, a fifth,
and watch them
burning
slowly
down to my fingers.

## VII.

I burn all of my shoes
and clothes
in the bathtub,
imagining that the fire
is eating my anger.

## VIII.

I take a knitting needle
to my towels.
I start to unravel my anger.

## IX.

I dye some milk with red food coloring.
I pour the milk in an ice cube tray
and put it in the freezer.
It will only take a few hours
to freeze my anger.

## X.

Naked, I sit in the window
of my third-story apartment,
unrolling countless rolls
of toilet paper
onto the darkened
lawn below.
When the sun comes
to reveal *me*
to the world,
I have only unrolled
a very small part
of my anger.

## The Mask

What is it made of, *papier-mâché*
or clay chalk-white and cold
a grave to put your face in

or is it coarse-weave linen
wetted and beaten
molded to a frame and meant
to resemble truth or beauty

It does resemble beauty

And what a thin skin—
it is delicate
almost transparent
and yet impregnable

What is it made of
shell or bone
a tusk carved out and hollow
more than a weapon

or the ash-grey dung of those
who've hurt you
mixed with the tears of those
you find reasons to hurt
compounded, shaped
smoothed, dried
hardened

# Oneself

A mirror is one side of the box One lives in.
The box is made of windows made of mirrors.
One's face, pressed up against the glass,
    as flat as a mirror is flat,
      does not see houses, willow trees,
      ducks on the far mirrored lake.
One does not see the random cars
    passing by One's house,
      does not see his own children
      burnished by the sun.
Beyond, beyond, the faceless ducks
    dive through the window of the lake,
      breaking down its opacity,
      splashing water into the sky like rain.
Sky is another side of One's box,
    as flat, as opaque as a mirror is opaque.
One watches television, talks at his wife.
One cannot see through the sky.

## One's Gift

On his birthday, One finds a box
    sitting on his doorstep,
    a box the shape of a cube
    wrapped in silver paper.
A card on top of the box reads
    simply: *to One from Anonymous.*
One opens the box as quickly as possible.
Inside the box is a jar.
Inside the jar is a face,
    nobody's face.
One studies the face
    but, before he can place it,
    the face begins to fade
    and disappears.
Instead of the face, One sees his own,
    nobody's.

# Shell

## I.

After the bell,
the fading bell,
last bell to be heard,
he walks the dark beaches,
far from the vain, curled alleys,
far from the world's grave sanity.
His ears have sealed their channels
to the silly ships of sound;
lights out, his eyes spiral inward
and madness wraps him
in a colored shroud.
The sea does not mourn him;
her dumb waves break
promises on the sand.

## II.

He notices nothing:
not how the moon pulls the sea up
like a chair and sits listening;
not how the insects curiously drone,
their eyes vague black questions;
not how the sharp-faced sands
lie gossiping;
not how the red horizon dies;
not how quietly the conch is waiting,
a dead, hushed bone.

The shell is cave-like, brooding and strange.
The shell is a blue, dead birthday in his hands.
It breathes a fossil breath,
breath of a cold womb.
It breathes of the primitive, buried rooms
of peaceful, muffed cities,
of the earth's great stone coffins,
the crystal coffins of ice.
Death is a worm
coiled like wire in its brain,
inceptive, a numb suggestion.

## III.

He wants to walk the shell's winding halls
down into darkness, into the bloodless cone,
to hide in its heart like a smothered crab,
preserved, unbothered, alone.
He digs his toes deeply into the sand
where they root like stones.
He slides his tongue over the shell-scales,
lizard-slick over the little nubs:
his tongue is a ruthless digger;
his tongue is a nailless, bleeding toe.

## IV

Now he lies like a wave
on the shifting sand,
his mouth on the shell's damp mouth.
At last he is close to *something:*
the thick salt air sticks like chalk to his skin;

the darkness is thin with the milk of stars;
the waves—and he is a wave—sink
down softly into sleep
and the seaweed stops tumbling;
the driftwood is greyer than wintered corpses;
the old sea moans and moans.
His heart beats the bars of night's padded cage:
greater than hope, this grave of groans.

## V.

The bridges of his nerves
have burned behind him: he feels nothing.
In his dark, earned corner, his painless plot,
he settles like a question Death has answered.
He wants nothing of morning's pale officers
or the blind understandings of sun-sane men.
He wants only to perish,
to stretch in the sand
like a black-tongued snake,
shedding his wretched inner skin.

# Childhood's End

Bulb by bulb the lights
burn out
in the fields.
Filaments wither;
the flowers wilt
on their stems.
In the cities
empty streets stretch out
in darkness
as one by one the streetlamps
blink, snap shut.
In darkness
a star like a rocket
falls and falls
for the sun is out,
burned out,
blind and still
in its socket.

## Falling in Caves

For years it had slept in Gregor's wood,
    stretched under boys and camp gear,
    yawning out its stale mouth
all the fears and dreams of our tomorrows.
I was a child then, ten years old
    by the sun's quick calendar,
    careless of slingshot and quail,
and when a hare shot into the wood
I was after it, feet sure as distance
    and the hidden mouth-yawn waiting
    for me under the leaves.
Falling,
      my feet chewed out from under me,
the dark wounds all around, my head bumped,
    my jeans ripped to skin-shreds,
    and I was inside down
on my knees, tearing out fistfuls of darkness.
My belt then, and the lucky flashlight trained
    on air and strange walls.
    *The walls!* There were bison
and great angry mastodons, wild boars ripping stone,
burning with hunt fevers; there were stick men
    with tiny slings and spears
    and fires to cook meat.
*They were alive.*
        I traced a boar's tusk
and felt its raw-bone hardness piercing my hand.
    I remember that feeling now,
    tracing your bone-white, curving thighs,

and I know we are as alive as
mastodons eternally dying on cave walls, alive as
    anything that struggles to survive.
    There in the cave's jaws
the first wheels started turning my head around.
They are turning still, down root-deep inside me,
    meshing time's slow, certain teeth.
    We are falling into forever,
and there's nothing to keep it from us.

## Ghost Town, Mill and White

Sun burns forests beyond the hill,
but here its fires are cold.
An old mill turns slowly.
Gently wind blows, rustling leaves,
and dusk wraps the wood in sheer scarves.
Birds nest in birches, thin-wristed, gashed;
birds freckle-feathered, their words a pulse.
Above me the insects are whirrs, noise;
their wings are white shadows.
A creek sings songs of rivers, rain,
of sea and smooth white stones.
Twigs are scattered bones on the banks,
on the swollen soil.
The wood is noisy, full of owls.
I lie on brown leaves, listening.
My hands are leaves;
my eyes are leaves.
Mushrooms push through my fingers,
raw, white, thirsty tongues.

# Nymph

I have come
with an earth smudge
on my nose

and wood words
under my tongue.
My eyes are

the dark elves
watching you sleep.
My fingers

are dotted
about your dreams
like watch lights

and candles.

## The Lamps of Night

Child, the lamps of night
burn brightly, softly, as you sleep,
though you in your bed of feathers
may not see them.

The night birds and the bats,
the soft grey feathered moths,
are diving through the streetlamps
as you sleep.

The stars are out now,
flying in circles,
and so are the fireflies,
flying in circles
of circles.

Glow worms lie
radiant under straw,
little curled fingers of light,
curled as the moon,
ringed in jewels,
secure in their beds
of straw and leaves
and feathers.

Out in the wood,
near a darkened pool,
stones that no one sees
are glowing,
golden.

There are others too,
enduring and subtle,
lamps of magic, elves' lamps,
lamps of dreams,
and the tiny lamps
the moon lights
on the leaves
of all the trees.

## Hide and Seek

One morning the sun did not rise
in the east as expected.
It rose through the roots of trees,
up through the trunks and branches
and into the leaves.
There the sun hid for a long time.
The earth did not know where the sun was hiding.
It looked high, then low, then high again.
The sun was not in the sky!
The earth ran around and around for hours
trying to find where the sun might be.
The sun was laughing all that time, disguised
as thousands and thousands of golden leaves.

# Acknowledgments

Grateful acknowledgment is made to the following publications in which these poems first appeared, some in earlier versions:

*AURA Literary/Arts Review:* "Oneself"
*Black Sun, New Moon:* "Fable for Fools," "Ghost Town, Mill and White"
*Bootlaig:* "Ten Vain Attempts"
*DeKalb Literary Arts Journal:* "Bare Feet: Europe in a Fit of Downs,"
    "Falling in Caves," "Father and Son," "Karen," "Nymph"
*Georgia State University Review:* "Shell"
*North Carolina SUN:* "The Lamps of Night," "The Mask"
*This Issue:* "On Bus With Bibleman"

The following poems have received awards or honorable mentions in juried competitions:

"Bare Feet: Europe in a Fit of Downs": first prize for poetry (Southern
    Literary Festival, University of Southern Mississippi, 1974)
"Father and Son": honorable mention for poetry (Agnes Scott College
    Literary Festival, 1974)
"Shell": second prize for poetry (Southern Literary Festival,
    University of Southern Mississippi, 1975)
"Nymph": selected to appear in *Who's Who Among Poets in American
    Colleges and Universities* (1976)

Grateful acknowledgement is made to the sponsors and judges of the above competitions for their interest in and support of the literary arts.

*Cover art, "Preserved in the Caves," by Mauro Moroni (Milan, ITA); cover and interior book design by Diane Kistner (dkistner@futurecycle.org); Gentium Book Basic with Fertigo Bold titling*

## About FutureCycle Press

FutureCycle Press is dedicated to publishing lasting English-language poetry and flash fiction books, chapbooks, and anthologies in both print-on-demand and ebook formats. Founded in 2007 by longtime independent editor/publishers and partners Diane Kistner and Robert S. King, the press incorporated as a nonprofit in 2012.
A number of our editors are distinguished poets and authors in their own right, and we have been actively involved in the small press movement going back to the early seventies.

The FutureCycle Poetry Book Prize and honorarium is awarded annually for the best full-length volume of poetry we publish in a calendar year. Introduced in 2013, our Good Works projects are devoted to issues of global significance, with all proceeds donated to a related worthy cause. We are dedicated to giving all authors we publish the care their work deserves, making our catalog of titles the most distinguished it can be, and paying forward any earnings to fund more great books.

We've learned a few things about independent publishing over the years. We've also evolved a unique, resilient publishing model that allows us to focus mainly on vetting and preserving for posterity the most books of exceptional quality without becoming overwhelmed with bookkeeping and mailing, fundraising activities, or taxing editorial and production "bubbles." To find out more about what we are doing, come see us at www.futurecycle.org.

www.ingramcontent.com/pod-product-compliance
Lightning Source LLC
Chambersburg PA
CBHW070117070426
42448CB00040B/3110